D1549266

5430000082960 5

ANTARCTICA

by

Grace Jones

Bracknell Forest
Borough Council
5430000082960 5
Askews & Holts

Image Credits
All images are courtesy of Shutterstock.com, unless otherwise specified. With thanks to Getty Images, Thinkstock Photo and iStockphoto.
Front Cover – MZPHOTO.CZ, Yann hubert, Neale Cousland. 1 – Li Hui Chen. 4&5 – DM7, Reinhold Leitner. 6&7 – PhilipYb Studio, Villiers Steyn, Morphart Creation, underworld. 8&9 – Li Hui Chen, Jan Miko. 10&11 – rm, Leksele, Achim Baque, Yann hubert, robert mcgillivray, Dmytro Pylypenko, Sergey 402. 12&13 – vladsilver, Denis Burdin, Dmytro Pylypenko. 14&15 – rm, TRphotos, Nightman1965, maplab (via Wikimedia Commons). 16&17 – Ritesh Chaudhary, hecke61. 18&19 – Anton_Ivanov, MZPHOTO.CZ, holbox. 20&21 – Paul S. Wolf, maplab (via Wikimedia Commons), Anne Powell, Joost van Uffelen. 22&23 – Andrew M. Allport, lovemelovemypic. 24&25 – koya979, Pressmaster, amophoto_au, Monkey Business Images, Naypong, gabriel12. 26&27 – 360b, Rawpixel.com, Wildnerdpix, Vladimir Melnik, Syda Productions, VILevi. 29 – Andrew Sutton.

BookLife
PUBLISHING

©2018
BookLife Publishing
King's Lynn
Norfolk PE30 4LS

All rights reserved.
Printed in Malaysia.

A catalogue record for this book is available from the British Library.

ISBN: 978-1-78637-243-7

Written by:
Grace Jones

Edited by:
Kirsty Holmes

Designed by:
Drue Rintoul

CONTENTS

Words that look like this are explained in the glossary on page 30.

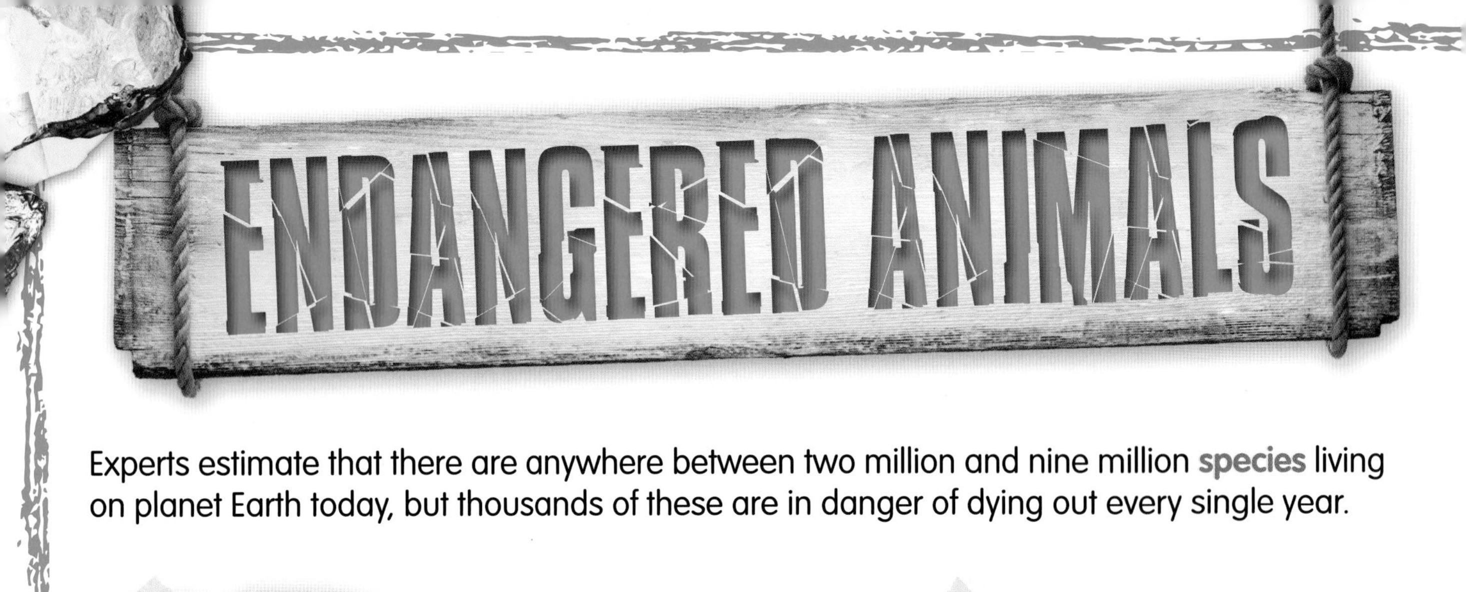

ENDANGERED ANIMALS

Experts estimate that there are anywhere between two million and nine million **species** living on planet Earth today, but thousands of these are in danger of dying out every single year.

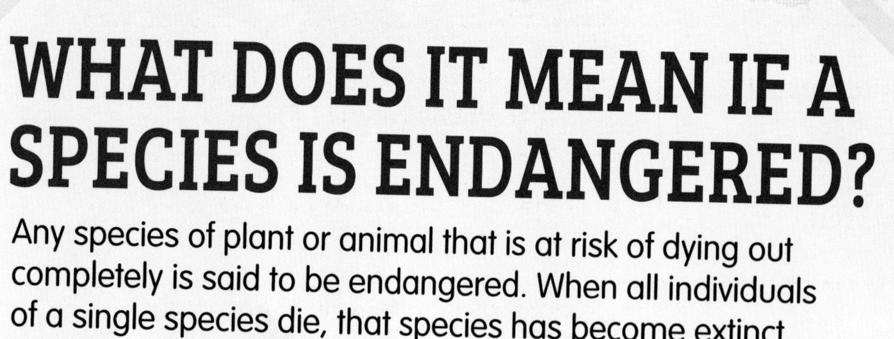

WHAT DOES IT MEAN IF A SPECIES IS ENDANGERED?

Any species of plant or animal that is at risk of dying out completely is said to be endangered. When all individuals of a single species die, that species has become extinct. Extinction is a real possibility for all species that are already threatened or endangered. Experts estimate that between 150 and 200 different species become extinct every day.

Dinosaurs are an example of an extinct species. They walked the Earth over 225 million years ago and became extinct around 65 million years ago.

The International Union for Conservation of Nature and Natural Resources (IUCN) is the main organisation that records which species are in danger of extinction. The species are put into different categories, from the most to the least threatened by extinction.

IUCN'S CATEGORIES OF THREATENED ANIMALS

Category	Explanation
Extinct	Species that have no surviving members
Extinct in the Wild	Species with only surviving members in captivity
Critically Endangered	Species that have an extremely high risk of extinction in the wild
Endangered	Species that have a high risk of extinction in the wild
Vulnerable	Species that are likely to become endangered or critically endangered in the near future
Near Threatened	Species that are likely to become vulnerable or endangered in the near future
Least Concern	Species that fit into none of the above categories

The Javan rhinoceros has been categorised by the IUCN as 'critically endangered', with around 46-66 individuals remaining in the wild.

The IUCN's work is extremely important. Once a species has been recognised as at risk, organisations and governments will often take steps to protect the species and its habitats in order to save it from extinction. The practice of protecting or conserving a species and its habitats is called conservation.

WHY DO ANIMALS BECOME ENDANGERED?

Over the last 100 years, the human **population** of the world has grown by over 4.5 billion people. As the population has grown, the damage humans do to the **environment** and wildlife has increased too. Many experts believe that human activity is the biggest threat to animals around the world today.

Habitat Destruction

One of the biggest threats species face is the loss of their habitats. Large areas of land are often used to build **settlements** to provide more housing, food and **natural resources** for the growing world population. This can often destroy natural habitats, which nearby wildlife need in order to survive.

To use land for housing or farming, all the trees must be cut down and cleared from the area. This is called **deforestation**.

POLLUTION

Pollution is the introduction of harmful waste to the air, water or land. Pollution threatens wildlife all over the world. For example, people drop litter, which can cut, choke or even poison animals.

Hunters and Poachers

Many species are endangered because of hunting or **poaching**. Humans throughout history have hunted certain species of animal for their meat, furs, skins or tusks.

Male African elephants are hunted by poachers for their huge tusks, which are made from a natural material called ivory and are sold for lots of money.

The dodo was a species of bird that was hunted to extinction. The last time a dodo was seen alive was in 1662.

GLOBAL WARMING

Earth's temperature is getting warmer at an extremely fast rate. This is mostly because of human activity. Humans have increasingly relied on **fossil fuels** for energy. When fossil fuels are burnt, they release **greenhouse gases** such as carbon dioxide.

When greenhouse gases are released into the air they trap heat in the Earth's **atmosphere**, making the planet warmer. This is called **global warming**. Global warming is having a big effect on the **polar regions**, as warmer temperatures have caused large areas of ice to melt. This has damaged the conditions that wildlife there – and around the world – need in order to survive.

The energy that is released when fossil fuels are burned is used to fuel cars, to run electricity plants and to heat our homes.

THE TEMPERATURE OF THE EARTH IS RISING AT NEARLY TWICE THE RATE IT WAS 50 YEARS AGO.

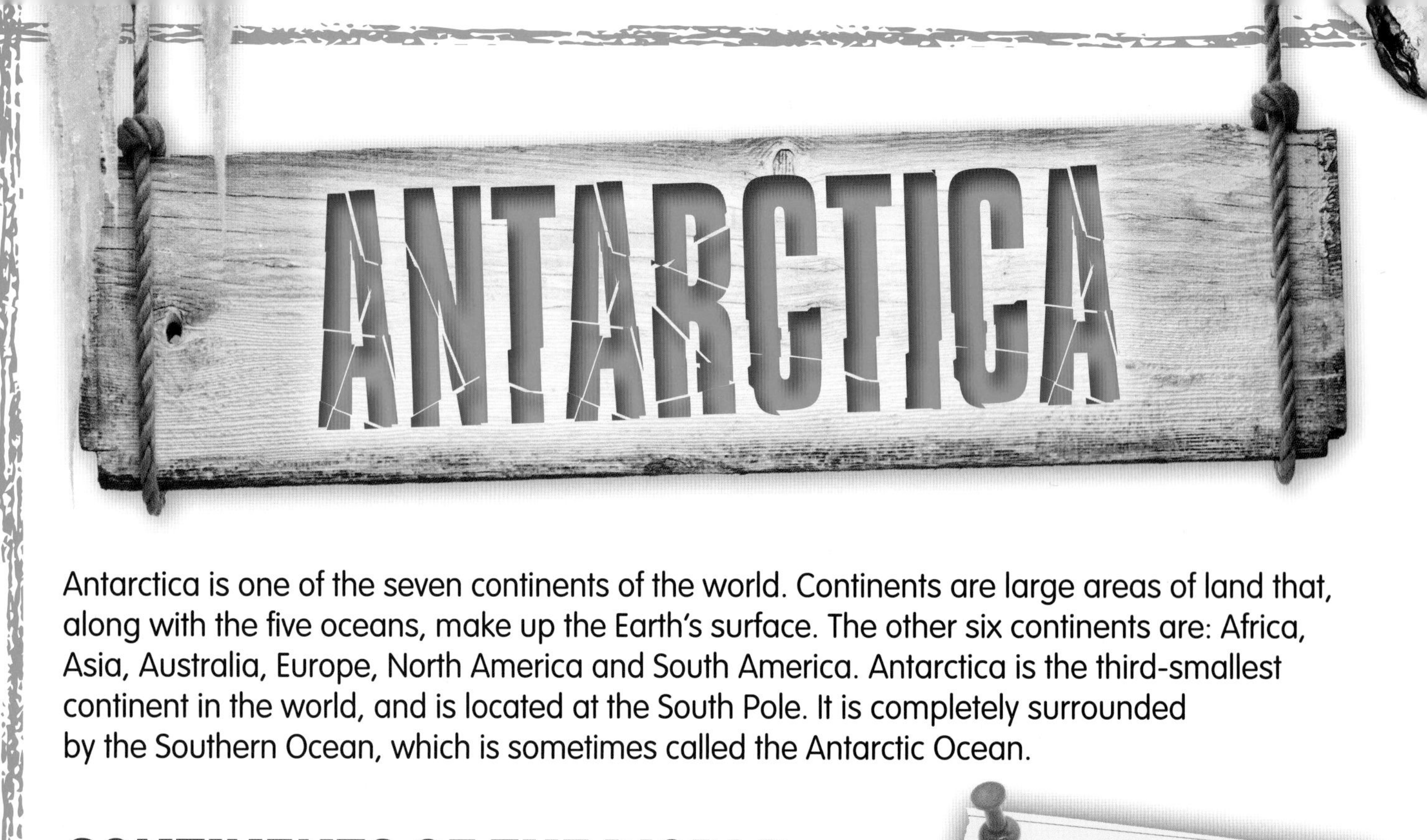

ANTARCTICA

Antarctica is one of the seven continents of the world. Continents are large areas of land that, along with the five oceans, make up the Earth's surface. The other six continents are: Africa, Asia, Australia, Europe, North America and South America. Antarctica is the third-smallest continent in the world, and is located at the South Pole. It is completely surrounded by the Southern Ocean, which is sometimes called the Antarctic Ocean.

CONTINENTS OF THE WORLD

DO YOU KNOW WHICH CONTINENT YOU LIVE IN?

ARCTIC OCEAN
NORTH AMERICA
EUROPE
ASIA
ATLANTIC OCEAN
PACIFIC OCEAN
AFRICA
PACIFIC OCEAN
SOUTH AMERICA
INDIAN OCEAN
AUSTRALIA
ANTARCTIC OCEAN (Southern Ocean)
ANTARCTICA

FACTS ABOUT ANTARCTICA

FACTFILE

Population: No people permanently live in Antarctica.

Land Area: Over 14 million square kilometres (km).

Countries: 0

Highest Peak: Mount Vinson is over 4,800 metres (m) above sea level.

Longest River: The Onyx river is around 32 km long.

Coldest Temperature: The coldest temperature ever recorded on Earth was −89.2 °C at Vostok Station in Antarctica.

Antarctica

Wildlife and Habitats

Antarctica is the coldest continent on Earth, with about 98% of its land covered in ice. Life in Antarctica can be very cold. The temperature usually never rises above 0°C, making it difficult for wildlife to survive. However, these landscapes are still home to a **diverse** range of wildlife, both on land and in the surrounding Southern Ocean.

An agreement between many countries bans anyone from touching the wildlife found in Antarctica.

ENDANGERED ANTARCTIC ANIMALS

Even though Antarctica has no people living on it permanently, the continent has still been affected by human activity. Global warming is the biggest threat to wildlife in Antarctica. Many species that live there rely on the sea ice to survive. As the planet warms up, and more sea ice melts, more species will be at risk of extinction.

10 ANIMALS IN DANGER IN ANTARCTICA

1

Southern Right Whale

Conservation Status:
Least Concern

Number:
Unknown. In 1997 there were around 7,500 southern right whales in the wild

2

Emperor Penguin

Conservation Status:
Near Threatened

Number:
595,000 adults living in the wild

3

Macaroni Penguin

Conservation Status:
Vulnerable

Number:
Around 12.6 million living in the wild

4

Blue Whale

Conservation Status:
Endangered

Number:
Between 10,000–25,000 living in the wild

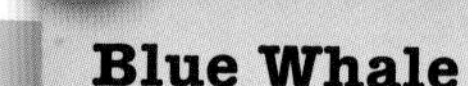

5

White-Chinned Petrel

Conservation Status:
Vulnerable

Number:
3,000,000 adults living in the wild

6

Leopard Seal

Conservation Status:
Least Concern

Number:
18,000 adults living in the wild

7

Humpback Whale

Conservation Status:
Least Concern

Number:
Unknown

8

Crab-Eater Seal

Conservation Status:
Least Concern

Number:
4,000,000 adults living in the wild

9

Antarctic Fur Seal

Conservation Status:
Least Concern

Number:
700,000–1,000,000 adults living in the wild

10

Ross Seal

Conservation Status:
Least Concern

Number:
40,000 adults living in the wild

EMPEROR PENGUIN

FACTFILE

Number Living in the Wild: 595,000 adults

IUCN Status: Near Threatened

Scientific Name: *Aptenodytes forsteri*

Weight: Between 22–45 kilograms (kg)

Size: Around 1.15 m tall

Life Span: Up to 60–70 years in the wild

Habitat: **Marine** habitats in Antarctic waters

Diet: **Carnivore**

Where Do They Live?

Emperor penguins live all over the Antarctic continent and feed in the surrounding Antarctic waters of the Southern Ocean. They have also been found in other countries close to Antarctica, such as Argentina, Chile and New Zealand.

Key

Oceans and Seas
Land
Emperor Penguin Habitats

WHY ARE THEY IN DANGER?

Because of global warming and rising temperatures, the sea ice in Antarctica has melted at an extremely quick rate. The melting sea ice has reduced the penguin's main food source, **krill**. Young krill feed off the algae that lives in the sea ice, so when the sea ice melts, the krill disappear and the emperor penguin's main food source disappears too. It is thought that the krill population has **decreased** by 80% in some areas of the Antarctic.

SOME SCIENTISTS BELIEVE THAT THE POPULATION OF EMPEROR PENGUINS COULD DECREASE BY AS MUCH AS TWO THIRDS BY THE YEAR 2100 BECAUSE OF GLOBAL WARMING.

How Are They Being Protected?

Currently, **conservationists** are calling for urgent action to help to save the emperor penguin. One suggestion is to create new **Marine Protected Areas** in order to protect krill from the effects of overfishing.

However, much more needs to be done to limit global warming if we are to stop the emperor penguins from becoming extinct in the near future.

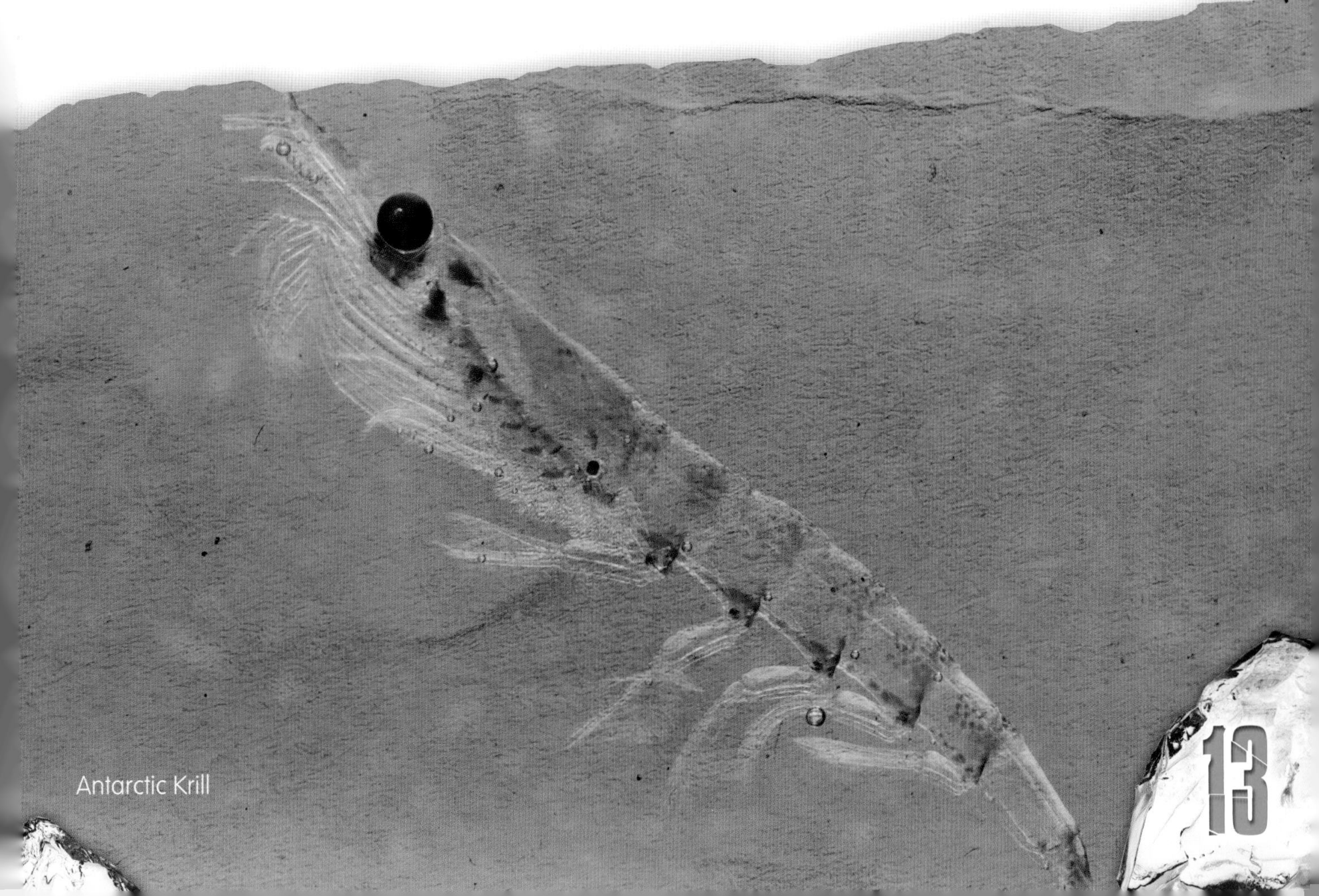

Antarctic Krill

BLUE WHALE

FACTFILE

Number Living in the Wild: Between 10,000–25,000

IUCN Status: Endangered

Scientific Name: *Balaenoptera musculus*

Weight: Can weigh over 180,000 kg. That's around the same as 100 cars!

Size: Can grow to lengths of over 30 m

Life Span: Between 80-90 years

Habitat: Ocean habitats throughout the world

Diet: Carnivore

Did you know that a blue whale's tongue can weigh as much as a whole elephant?

Where Do They Live?

Blue whales are found in three main locations; the North Atlantic Ocean, the North Pacific Ocean and the Southern **Hemisphere**. They **migrate** huge distances across each ocean spending summers in Antarctic and Arctic waters, and winters near the **Equator** where it's warm.

Key

- Areas where blue whale populations are not found
- Land
- Blue Whale Habitats

Why Are They in Danger?

In the first 60 years of the 20th century, blue whales were hunted for their oil, which was used to light oil lamps. Although replacements to whale oil were found, the species has never fully recovered from this hunting. By 1996, the number of Antarctic blue whales had dropped from 239,000 to only 1,700.

EVERY YEAR, MANY BLUE WHALES ARE KILLED FROM COLLISIONS WITH LARGE SHIPS.

HOW ARE THEY BEING PROTECTED?

The International Whaling Commission (IWC) aims to protect whales and other marine animals. They made the hunting of blue whales **illegal** in 1966. Since then, populations have shown some signs of recovery and on average the Antarctic population is increasing by 7.3% every year. There are also conservation efforts underway to find out more about the migration routes used by the blue whale. This will help create more Marine Protected Areas, which will limit the number of whales being killed by large ships.

NOT EVERY COUNTRY IN THE WORLD FOLLOWS IWC LAWS. FOR EXAMPLE, JAPAN AND RUSSIA CONTINUE TO HUNT WHALES.

Large Container Ship

LEOPARD SEAL

FACTFILE

Number Living in the Wild: 18,000 adults

IUCN Status: Least Concern

Scientific Name: *Hydrurga leptonyx*

Weight: Up to 450 kg

Size: Up to 3.6 m long

Life Span: 26 or more years

Habitat: Marine habitats around Antarctica

Diet: Carnivore

Leopard Seal

Where Do They Live?

Leopard seals mostly live in the waters around Antarctica in the Southern Hemisphere.

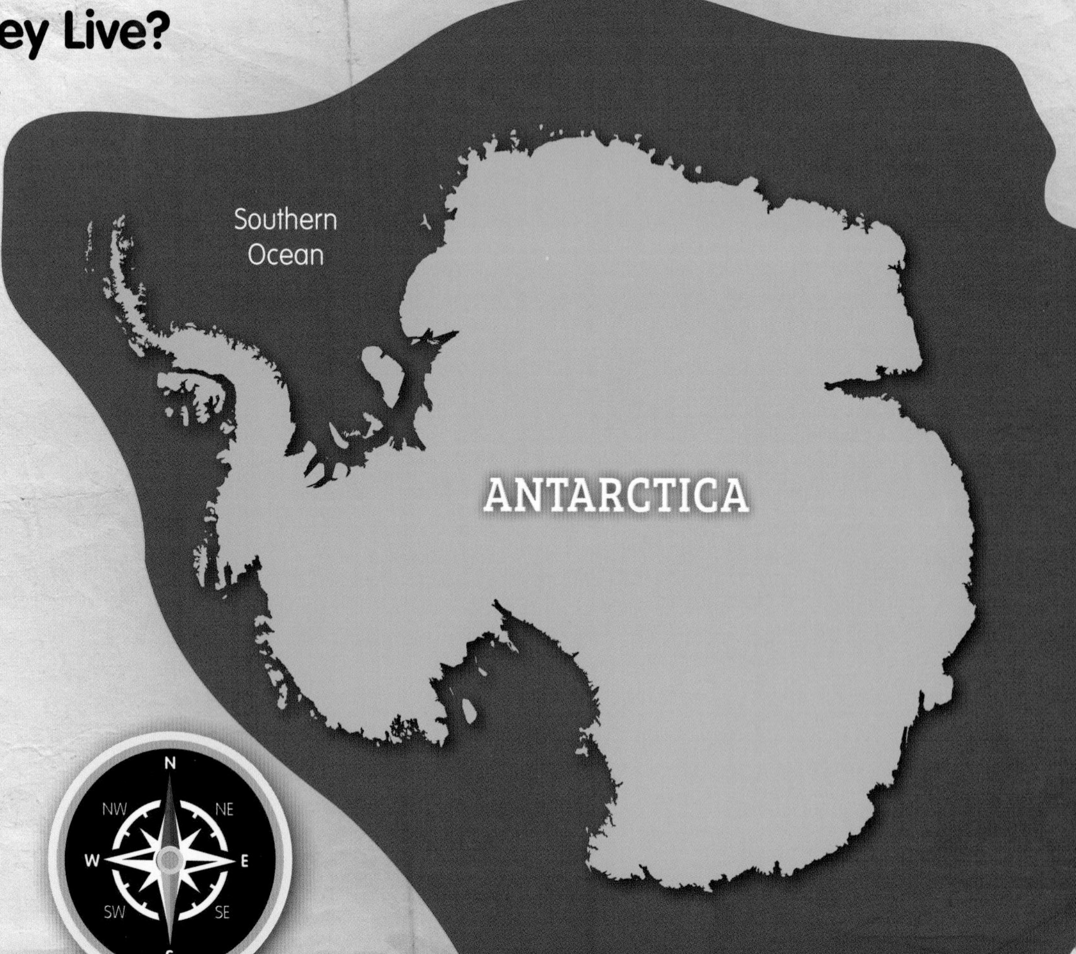

Key

Oceans and Seas

Land

Leopard Seal Habitats

Leopard seals use sea ice to give birth, raise their pups, rest and avoid other **predators**. The melting sea ice affects their food source, andthe habitats where they raise their pups. Both of these things affect the leopard seal's **survival rate**.

WHY ARE THEY IN DANGER?

Even though leopard seals are not listed as threatened, their population is thought to have decreased by over a quarter of a million in the last 40 years. It is not known exactly why this is the case, but it is thought that global warming is partly responsible. Like the emperor penguin, the leopard seal's main food source is krill, which is also under threat. They also eat penguins and other seals, all of which eat krill. If the number of krill continues to decrease it will continue to affect the **survival rate** of leopard seals for years to come.

How Are They Being Protected?

Since 1972, it has been illegal to catch and kill seals under the Antarctic Treaty, and the Convention for the Conservation of Antarctic Seals. In order to protect the leopard seal, and other species in Antarctica, more conservation measures are needed to conserve the krill. There are many krill fisheries in the Antarctic, and some countries are looking to start even more. In order to save the leopard seal from becoming threatened in the future, countries need to work together to stop this practice.

Antarctic Krill

MACARONI PENGUIN

FACTFILE

Number Living in the Wild: Around 12.6 million

IUCN Status: Vulnerable

Scientific Name: *Eudyptes chrysolophus*

Weight: Around 5 kg

Size: Around 65 centimetres (cm) tall

Life Span: Around 12 years in the wild

Habitat: Marine habitats

Diet: Carnivore

Macaroni Penguin

Where Do They Live?

Macaroni penguins live in large groups called colonies. They live in and around the oceans surrounding countries in the Southern Hemisphere, including Antarctica, Chile and South Africa.

Key

Oceans and Seas

Land

Macaroni Penguin Habitats

ANTARCTICA

Why Are They in Danger?

The population of macaroni penguins has decreased by an estimated 30% over the past few decades. This is mainly because of the effects of **commercial fishing**. Some fisheries use nets that Macaroni penguins get caught up in. When tangled, they can't get to the surface to take a breath. Penguins are also losing their sea ice habitats, and their main food source, krill.

HOW ARE THEY BEING PROTECTED?

Conservation efforts have focused on the study and research of several macaroni penguin populations to better understand how to protect them. Conservationists are also trying to find out what damage commercial fisheries are causing by studying krill numbers and the numbers of penguins being killed by fishing nets. Conservationists hope that through understanding the effects they can change practices and save the macaroni penguin from extinction.

HUMPBACK WHALE

FACTFILE

Number Living in the Wild: Unknown

IUCN Status: Least Concern

Scientific Name: *Megaptera novaeangliae*

Weight: Around 40,000 kg

Size: Between 14–19 m long

Life Span: Between 40–100 years in the wild

Habitat: Ocean habitats throughout the world

Diet: Carnivore

Humpback Whale

Where Do They Live?

Like blue whales, humpback whales are found all over the world and migrate huge distances between summer and winter. Many humpback whales spend their summers around Antarctica and migrate towards the warmer waters near the Equator in winter.

Key

- Areas where humpback whale populations are not found
- Land
- Humpback Whale Habitats

WORLD MAP

WHY ARE THEY IN DANGER?

Humpback whales were hunted to near-extinction in the early and middle 20th century for their oil and meat. Since the early 20th century, around 220,000 humpback whales have been hunted in the Southern Hemisphere. In the 1950s and 1960s, hunting humpback whales became illegal. Humpback whales are one species of whale that has managed to recover slightly in recent years, although not to their original numbers.

Humpback whales can be killed accidentally by colliding with ships.

How Are They Being Protected?

The IWC has protected humpback whales since 1955 in the North Atlantic Ocean, 1963 in the Southern Hemisphere and 1966 in the North Pacific Ocean. Over the last 40 years, humpback whales have increased from a few thousand to 70,000. Thanks to international conservation, their numbers continue to increase.

WHITE-CHINNED PETREL

FACTFILE

Number Living in the Wild: 3,000,000 adults

IUCN Status: Vulnerable

Scientific Name: *Procellaria aequinoctialis*

Weight: Between 1–1.9 kg

Wingspan: Between 1.3–1.5 m wide

Life Span: Can live for over 30 years

Habitat: Marine habitats

Diet: Carnivore

White-Chinned Petrel

Where Do They Live?

White-chinned petrels live in marine and coastal habitats across the Southern Hemisphere, especially on islands within the Southern Ocean.

Key

- Oceans and Seas
- Land
- White-Chinned Petrel Habitats

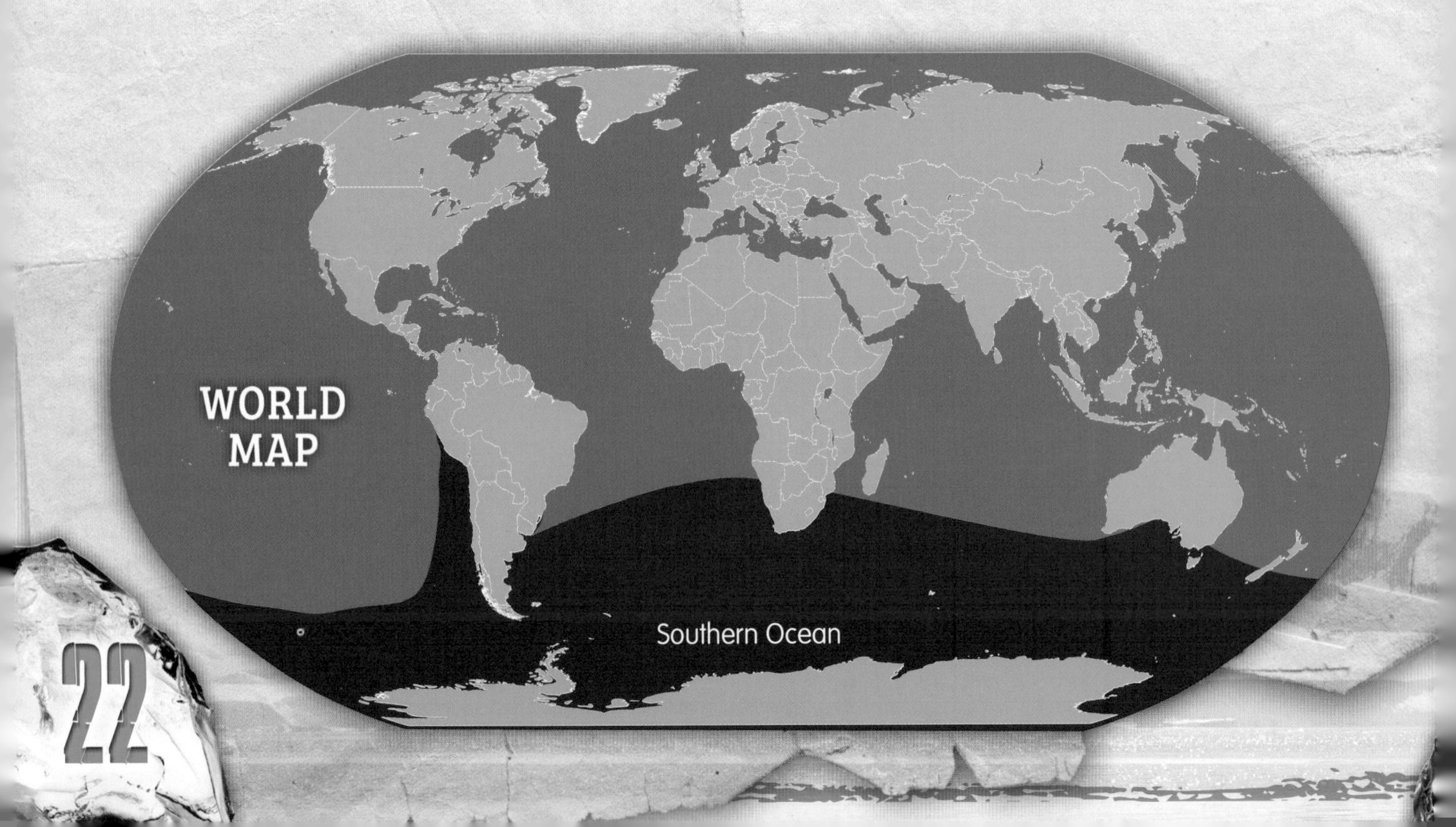

Why Are They in Danger?

White-chinned petrels are threatened by commercial fisheries. Large numbers are becoming tangled in a type of fishing net called a longline net. They try to eat the bait hooked on the line and can easily swallow the hooks. When they become caught on the hook they are often pulled down under the water and drown. At a few of their main **breeding** locations, such as the Crozet and South Georgia Islands, their eggs and chicks are often eaten by rats.

Longline fishing hooks, that are responsible for the deaths of many white-chinned petrels.

ACAP aims to stop populations of 28 species of bird in the Southern Hemisphere from declining.

HOW ARE THEY BEING PROTECTED?

The white-chinned petrel is protected under the Agreement on the Conservation of Albatrosses and Petrels (ACAP). ACAP have created a conservation plan to stop longline fishing deaths and to protect habitats. The plan includes scaring away birds from longline nets and making sure the nets are released underwater to keep bait out of reach.

Many steps have already been taken to protect wildlife and conserve habitats throughout Antarctica, but much more can be done to save endangered animals from extinction.

Tackling Global Warming

Global warming is the single biggest threat that wildlife and humans face today, not just in Antarctica, but all around the world. In 2015, at the Paris Climate Conference, 195 countries met and agreed to the first ever global climate agreement. The agreement set out a global action plan to avoid dangerous climate change and limit global warming.

THE AGREEMENT

Amongst many other things, all 195 countries agreed to:

- Keep the global average temperature from rising by more than 2°C
- Significantly reduce the amount of carbon dioxide released into the atmosphere
- Create their own national action plans to tackle climate change
- Limit any increase in global average temperature to 1.5°C so that the risks of global warming are significantly reduced

With these measures in place, conservationists hope that the damage global warming is doing to the environment and wildlife will be reduced, and many species may even be saved from extinction.

WHAT YOU CAN DO TO HELP

1. WALK OR RIDE A BIKE TO SCHOOL INSTEAD OF TRAVELLING BY CAR OR BUS.

2. USE ENERGY-SAVING LIGHT BULBS OR EVEN LIGHTS THAT ARE POWERED BY THE SUN.

3. TURN OFF AND UNPLUG ELECTRONIC DEVICES SUCH AS TELEVISIONS OR LIGHTS WHEN YOU'RE NOT USING THEM.

4. SAVE WATER BY TURNING OFF THE TAP WHILE YOU ARE BRUSHING YOUR TEETH OR WASHING DISHES IN THE SINK.

5. RECYCLE OR REUSE PACKAGING AND MATERIALS SUCH AS PAPER AND GLASS.

HOW CAN I MAKE A DIFFERENCE?

1 CAMPAIGN WITH AN ORGANISATION

Wildlife organisations such as WWF and Greenpeace have helped to save many endangered species and even convince countries to change the laws through campaigning.

2 DONATE TO A CHARITY YOU BELIEVE IN

You can usually donate as little or as much as you want and most charities show you how your donations are helping to make a difference.

3 LEARN MORE ABOUT ENDANGERED SPECIES IN YOUR AREA

One of the most important ways to protect endangered species is by understanding the threats that they face. Visit a local wildlife refuge, national park or reserve or join a local wildlife organisation.

4 ADOPT AN ANIMAL

Your donation will normally go to feeding and looking after the animal that you have adopted. You'll usually get an adoption certificate and regular updates on how your animal is doing.

5 HELP TO RAISE AWARENESS BY TALKING TO OTHERS

It is important that we all talk about issues that may threaten wildlife throughout the world. By talking about these issues, it can help to make people aware of how they may be affecting wildlife and how they can help.

6 VOLUNTEER AT A LOCAL WILDLIFE CHARITY OR SHELTER

It is not only endangered animals who need our help. We should help to care for all the animals in the world.

FIND OUT MORE

To find out more about endangered species in Antarctica and what you can do to get involved with conservation efforts, visit:

Antarctic and Southern Ocean Coalition
www.asoc.org/advocacy/antarctic-wildlife-conservation

International Union for Conservation of Nature (IUCN)
www.iucnredlist.org

World Wide Fund for Nature (WWF)
www.worldwildlife.org

To discover more about other endangered animals around the world take a look at more books in this series:

Asia, Endangered Animals
Grace Jones (BookLife, 2018)

North America, Endangered Animals
Grace Jones (BookLife, 2018)

Australia, Endangered Animals
Grace Jones (BookLife, 2018)

Africa, Endangered Animals
Grace Jones (BookLife, 2018)

Europe, Endangered Animals
Grace Jones (BookLife, 2018)

South America, Endangered Animals
Grace Jones (BookLife, 2018)

1. HOW MANY WHITE-CHINNED PETRELS ARE LIVING IN THE WILD?

2. WHAT IS THE SCIENTIFIC NAME OF THE MACARONI PENGUIN?

3. WHAT DO EMPEROR PENGUINS MAINLY FEED ON?

4. HOW MUCH DOES A HUMPBACK WHALE WEIGH?

5. HOW LONG DO LEOPARD SEALS USUALLY LIVE?

6. WHAT IS THE IUCN CONSERVATION STATUS OF THE BLUE WHALE?

For answers see the bottom of page 32.

GLOSSARY

atmosphere	the mixture of gases that make up the air and surround the Earth
breeding	the process of producing young
captivity	animals that are cared for by humans and not living in the wild
carnivore	animals that eat other animals rather than plants
commercial fishing	fishing companies who make money from large-scale fishing
conservation	the practice of protecting or conserving a species and its habitats
conservationists	people who act for the protection of wildlife and the environment
decreased	made smaller in size or fewer in amount
diverse	lots of different types
environment	the natural world
Equator	the imaginary line around the Earth that is an equal distance from the North and South Poles
fossil fuels	fuels, such as coal, oil and gas, that formed millions of years ago from the remains of animals and plants
global warming	an increase in the Earth's temperature that causes changes in climate

governments	groups of people with the authority to run countries and decide their laws
greenhouse gases	gases that help to cause global warming such as carbon dioxide and methane
habitats	the natural environments in which animals or plants live
hemisphere	one of two halves of the Earth, especially above or below the Equator
illegal	forbidden by law
krill	small shrimp-like fish
marine	relating to the sea
Marine Protected Areas	protected areas of seas, oceans or large lakes usually for conservation purposes
migrate	to move from one place to another usually based on seasonal changes
natural resources	useful materials that are created by nature
poaching	the act of the illegal capturing or killing of wild animals
polar regions	the regions surrounding the north and south poles in the Arctic and Antarctic circles
population	the number of people living in a place
predators	animals that hunt other animals for food
settlements	places people live permanently, like villages or towns
species	a group of very similar animals or plants that are capable of producing young together
survival rate	the percentage of members of a species that survive

INDEX

1. Around 3,000,000 **2.** Eudyptes chrysolophus **3.** Krill **4.** Around 40,000 kilograms **5.** 26 or more years **6.** Endangered